Wheels

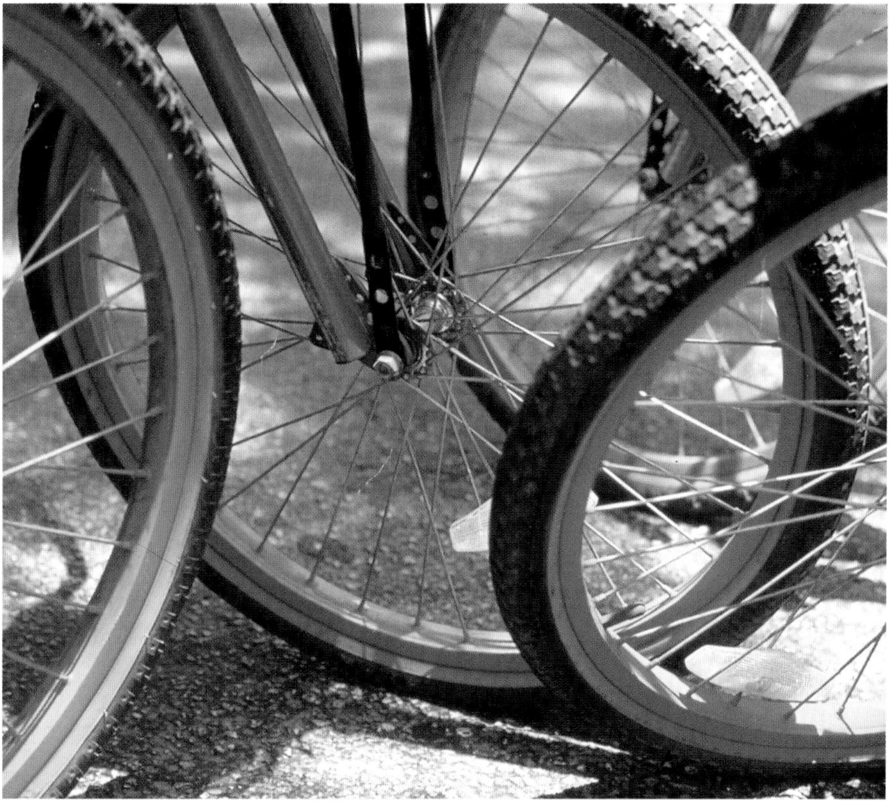

Brenda Parkes

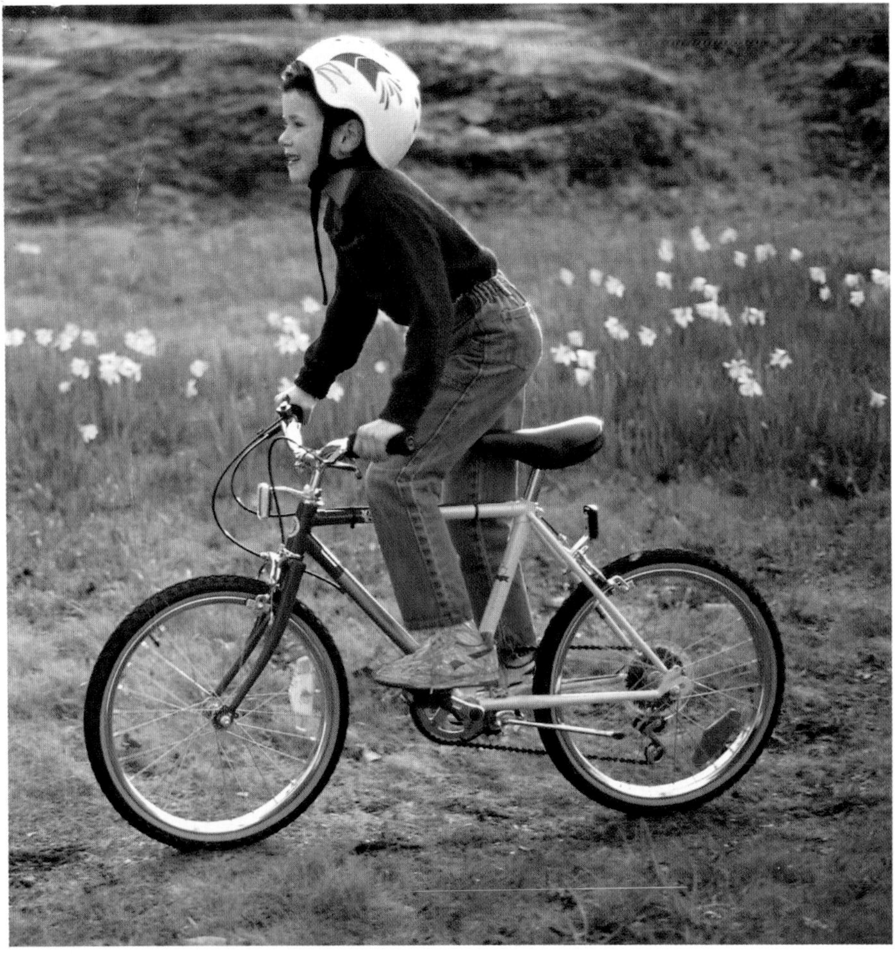

Wheels on a bike,

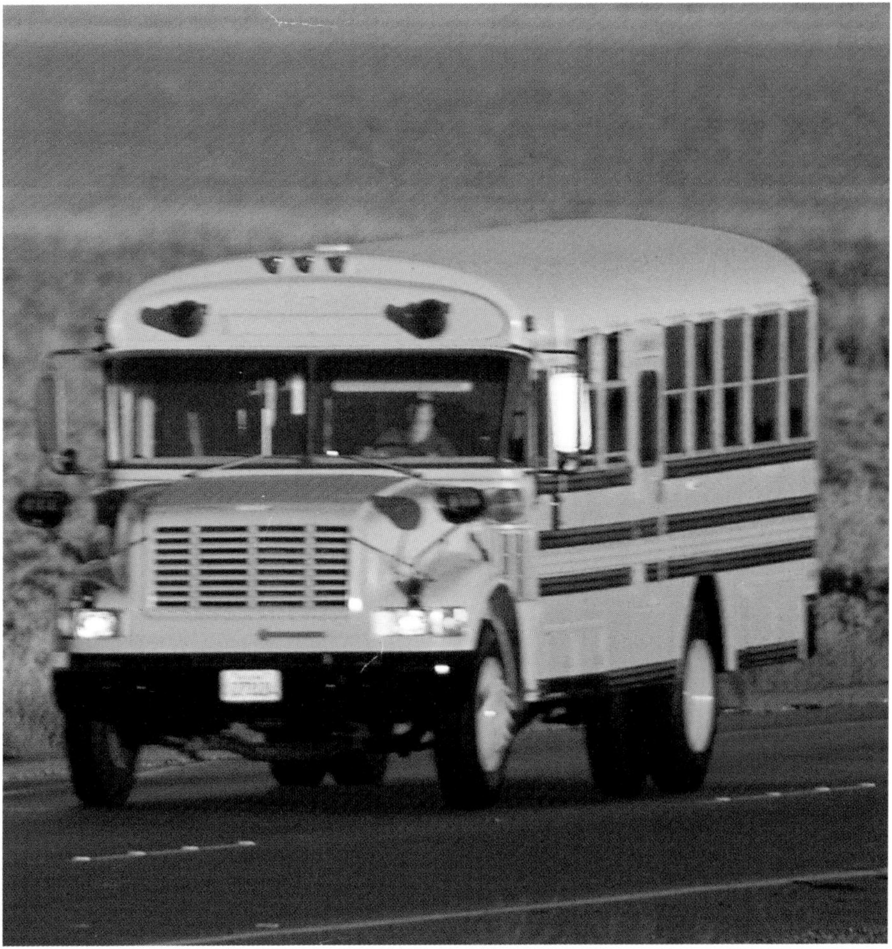

wheels on a bus,

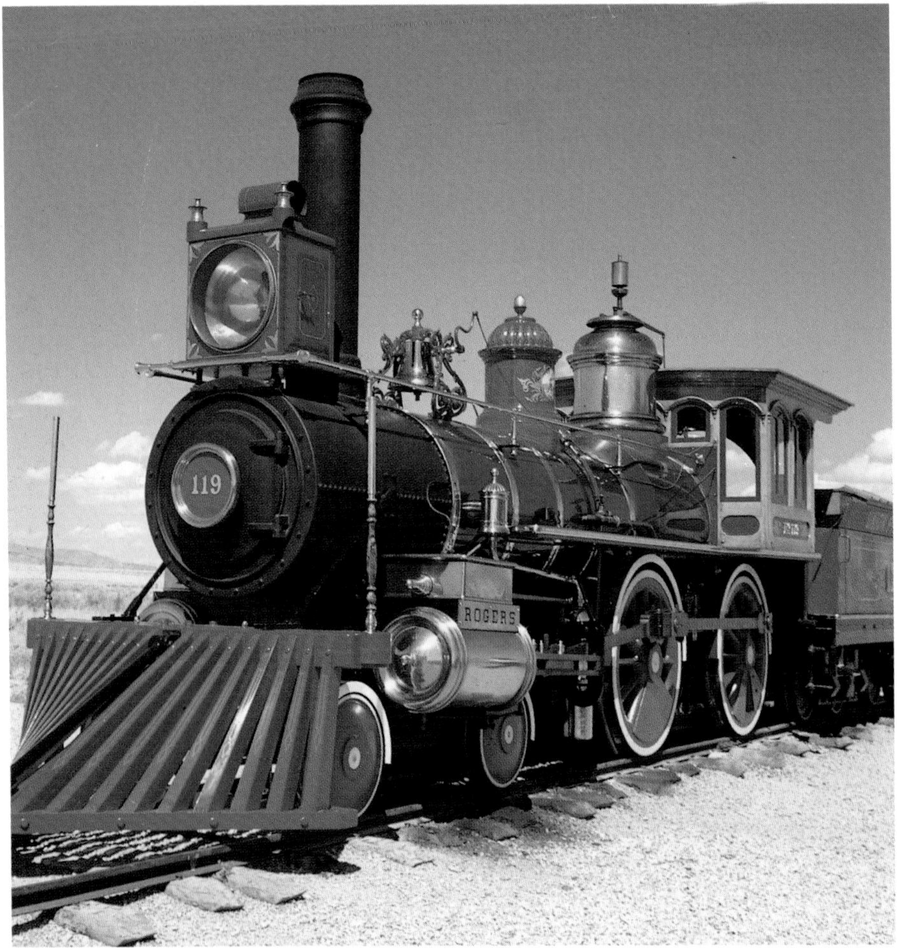

wheels on a train,

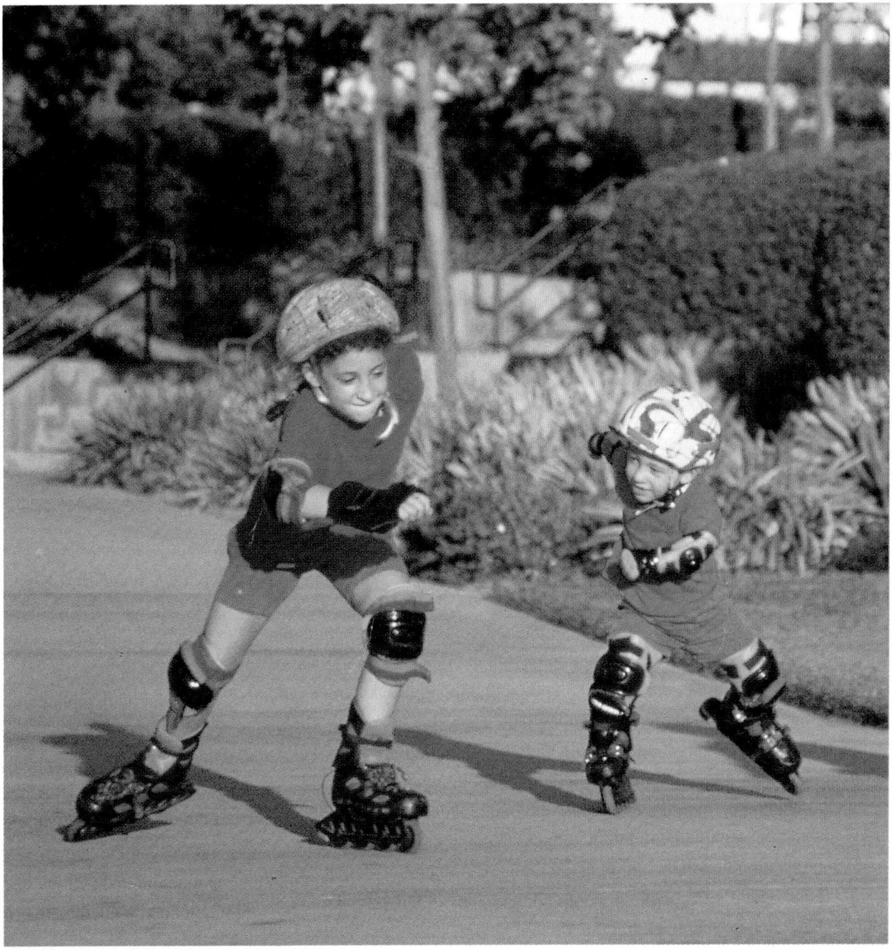

wheels on us,

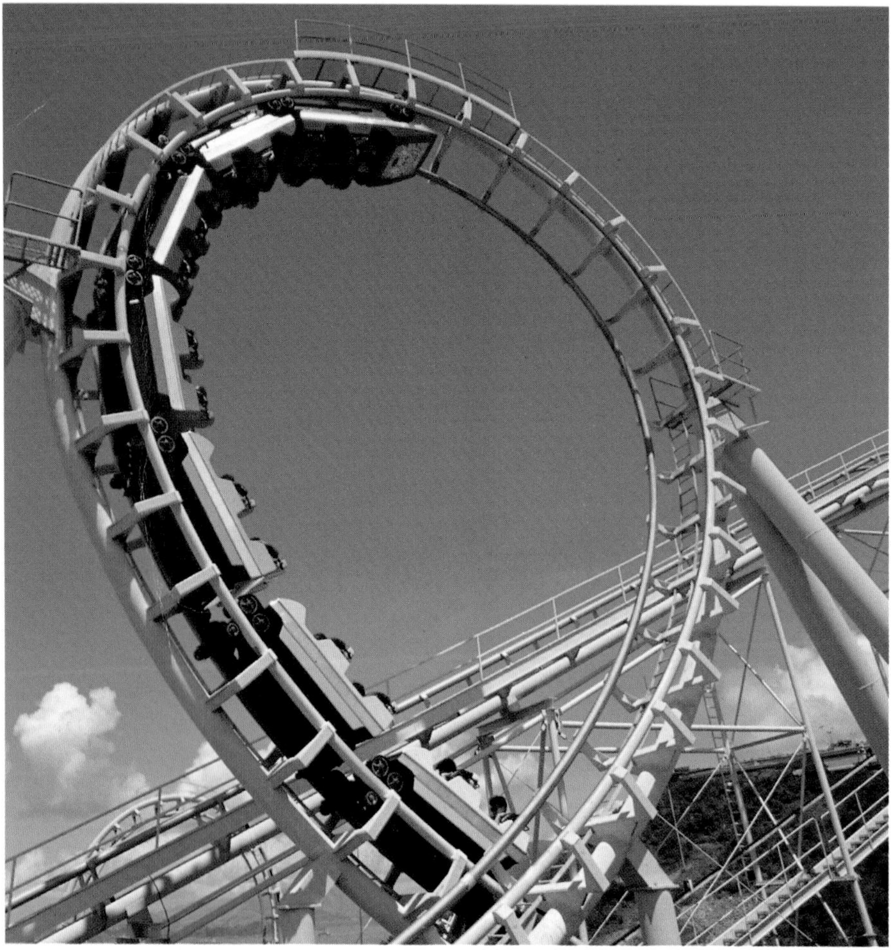

wheels on a track,

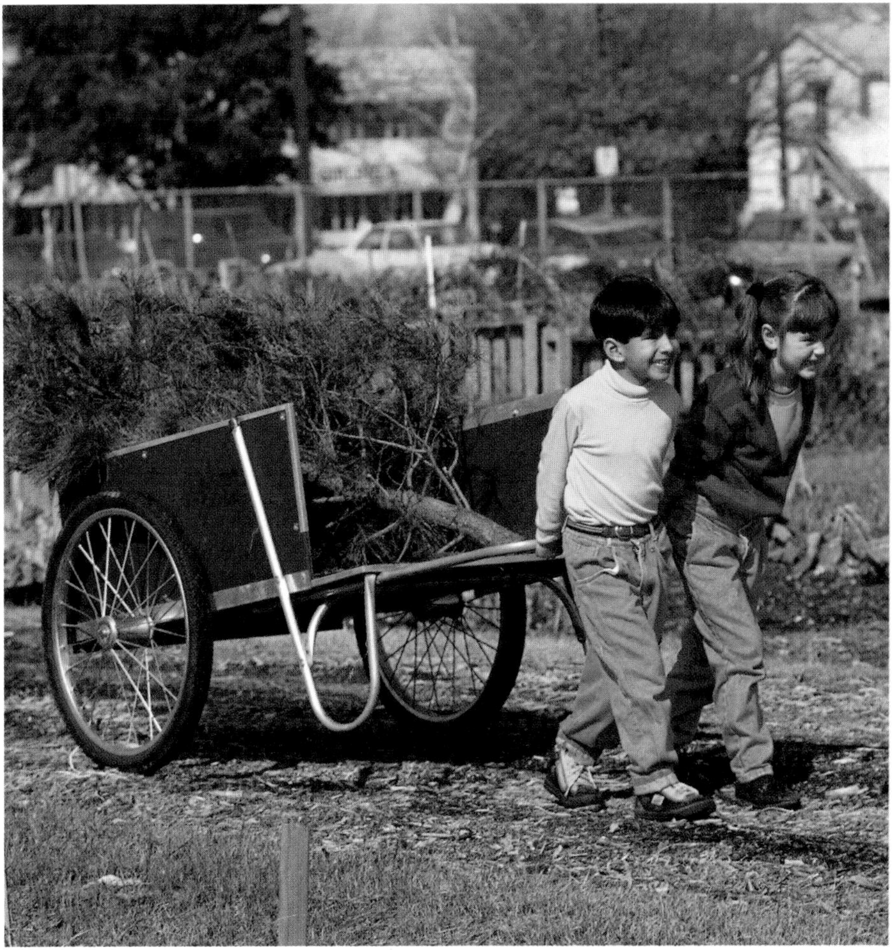

and wheels on the ground.

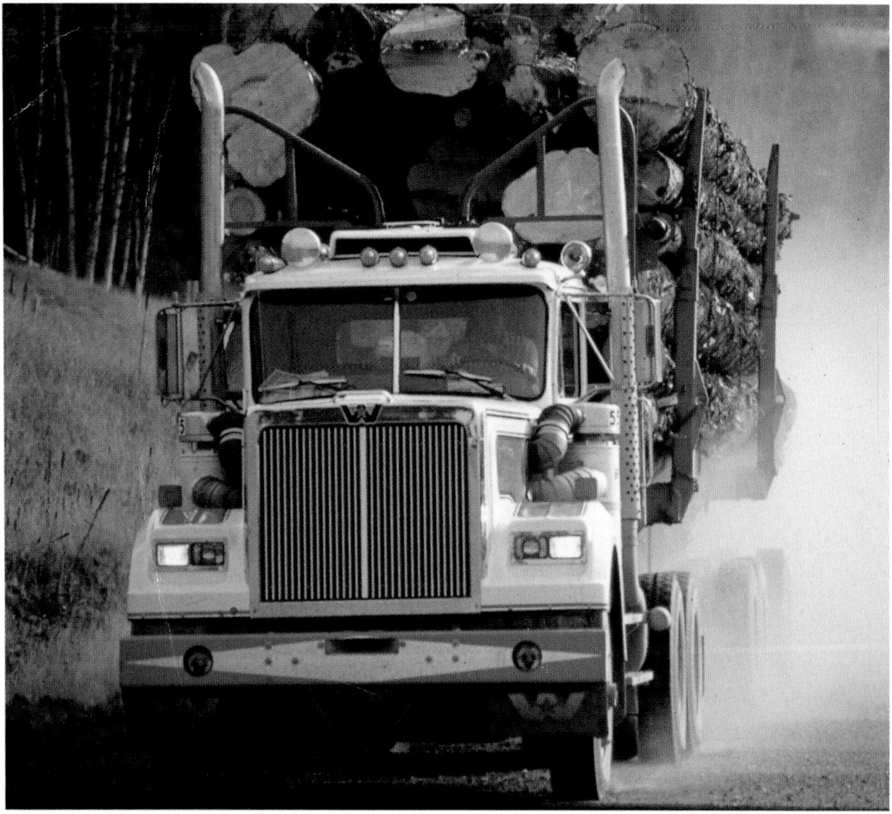

Wheels move many things around.